Contents

Bony bodies

LONG bones, SHORT bones, FLAT bones, curvy bones – the bones in our bodies come in all shapes and sizes. Together, they make our skeleton, our body's bony frame.

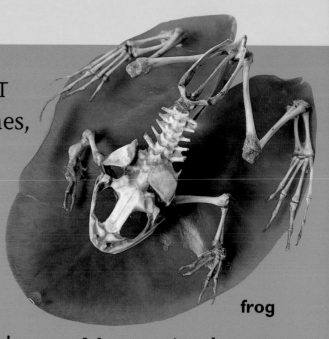

frog

Many animals, including humans, have bony skeletons. We all belong to a group of animals called vertebrates.

hamster

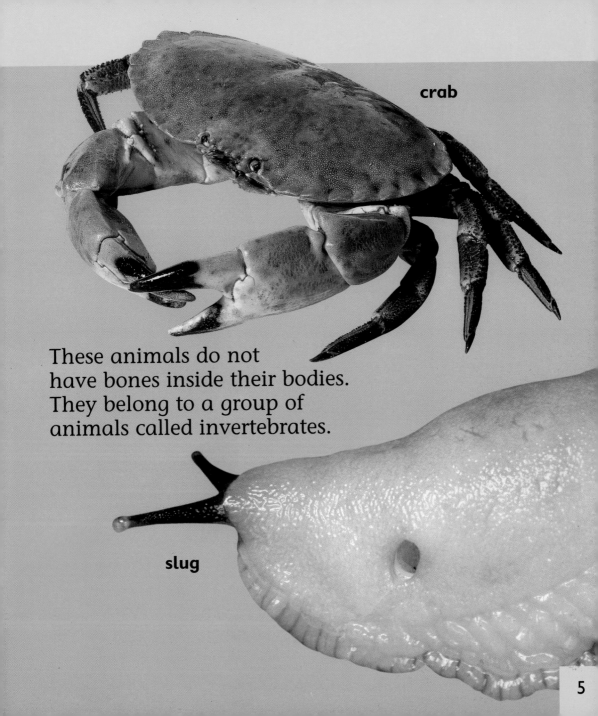

crab

These animals do not
have bones inside their bodies.
They belong to a group of
animals called invertebrates.

slug

Hard and strong

The skeleton is very important. This **strong**, bony frame supports the body and gives it its special shape.

A tent needs a framework to support it.

Your body needs one, too.

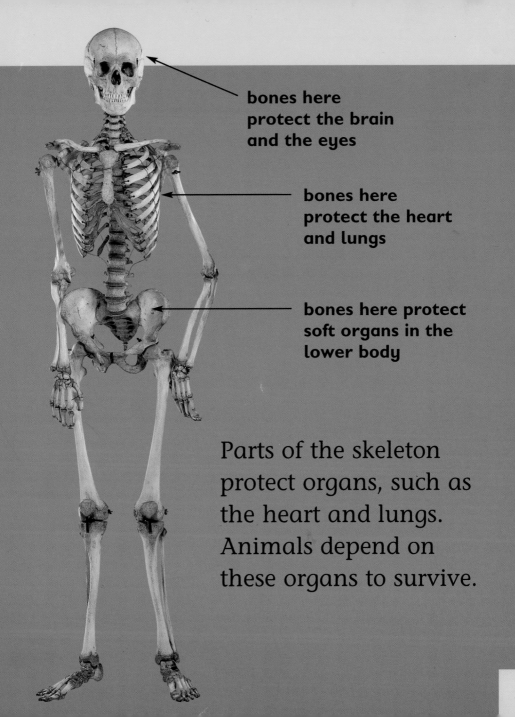

bones here protect the brain and the eyes

bones here protect the heart and lungs

bones here protect soft organs in the lower body

Parts of the skeleton protect organs, such as the heart and lungs. Animals depend on these organs to survive.

On the move

A skeleton helps an animal to move. The bones are connected to powerful muscles. When the muscles pull on the bones, the body starts to move.

The skeleton can only move where two bones meet. These parts of the skeleton are called joints.

An orang-utan's shoulder joints allow its arms to stretch and swing.

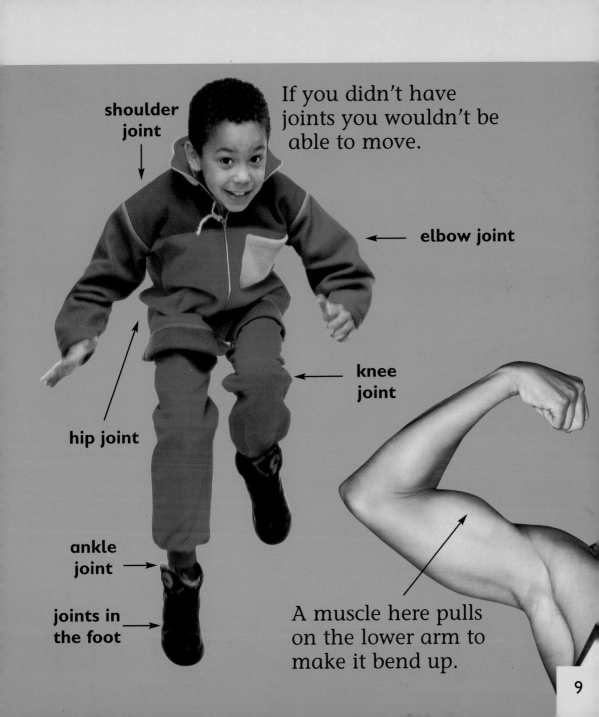

shoulder joint

If you didn't have joints you wouldn't be able to move.

elbow joint

knee joint

hip joint

ankle joint

joints in the foot

A muscle here pulls on the lower arm to make it bend up.

9

Animal skeletons

An animal's skeleton can tell you a lot about its life. The size and shape of the bones can show you how it moved, where it lived, and what it ate.

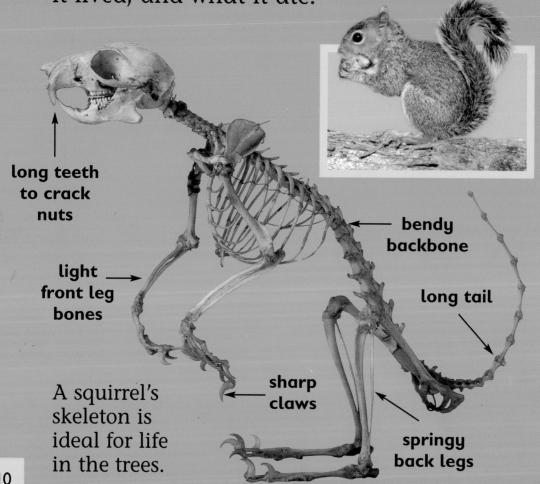

long teeth to crack nuts

light front leg bones

bendy backbone

long tail

sharp claws

A squirrel's skeleton is ideal for life in the trees.

springy back legs

This x-ray photo shows a snake's backbone. It is made up of lots of tiny bones, which can bend and curve like a chain.

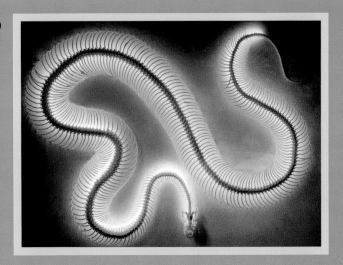

A fish's skeleton is perfect for moving through water.

stiff fins help fish to turn and stay upright

strong tail fin

long, bendy backbone

The human skeleton

The human skeleton has more than 200 bones, and they all have a special name.

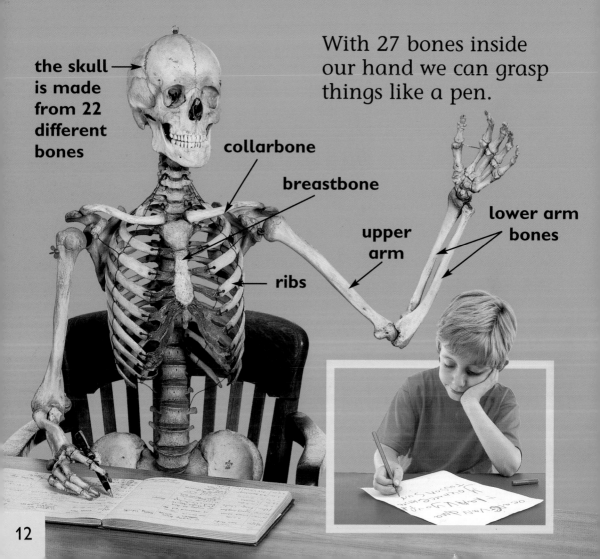

With 27 bones inside our hand we can grasp things like a pen.

the skull is made from 22 different bones

collarbone

breastbone

lower arm bones

upper arm

ribs

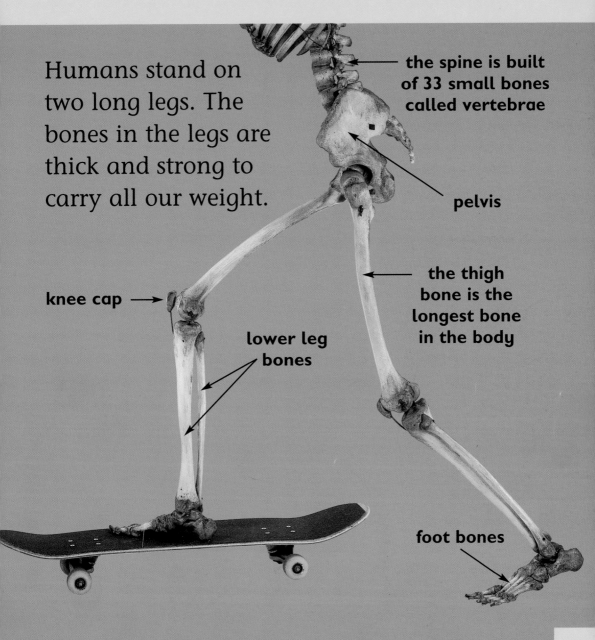

Humans stand on two long legs. The bones in the legs are thick and strong to carry all our weight.

the spine is built of 33 small bones called vertebrae

pelvis

the thigh bone is the longest bone in the body

knee cap →

lower leg bones

foot bones

Looking at skulls

The skull protects the brain, eyes, ears, nose and tongue. It is made up of 22 different bones, which join together when we are young.

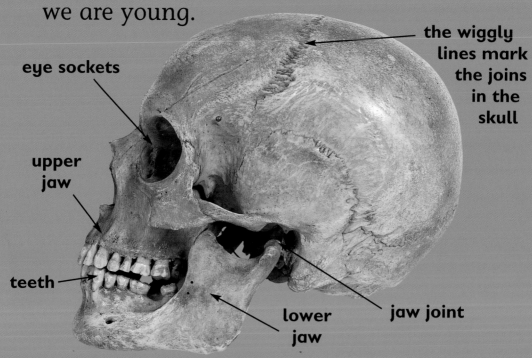

eye sockets

the wiggly lines mark the joins in the skull

upper jaw

teeth

lower jaw

jaw joint

The lower jaw is the skull's only moving part. The jaws help an animal to eat food. The **strong** teeth help to break it down.

A deer's narrow skull can reach the grass in every nook and cranny.

bony antlers

sharp front teeth cut grass

flat back teeth chew grass

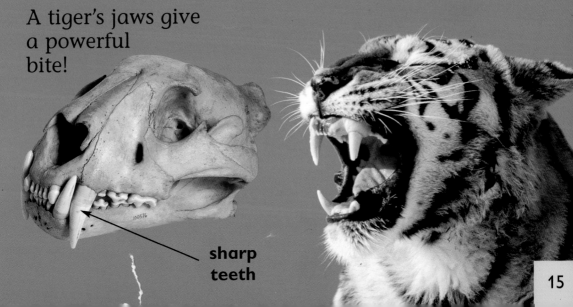

A tiger's jaws give a powerful bite!

sharp teeth

What is bone?

Bone is a strong, LIGHT material, which stands up well to wear and tear. Living bone is always changing, and can replace itself with brand new bone.

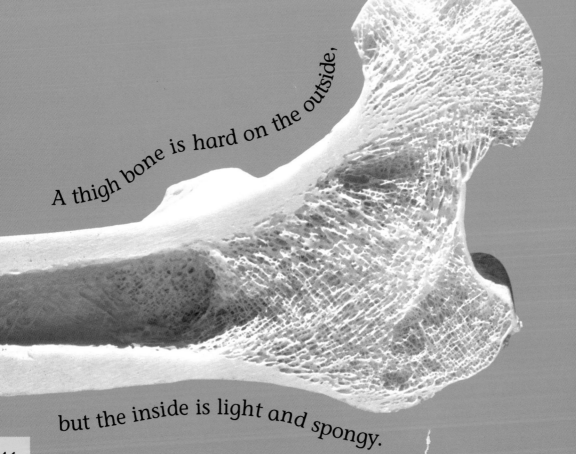

A thigh bone is hard on the outside, but the inside is light and spongy.

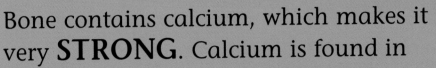

Bone contains calcium, which makes it
very **STRONG**. Calcium is found in
milk and cheese –
so, if you want
strong bones,
have plenty!

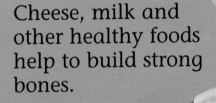

Cheese, milk and
other healthy foods
help to build strong
bones.

Breaking and mending

Have you ever broken a bone? Broken bones can mend themselves by simply growing back together.

The two ends need to be held in place so that the bone grows straight and **strong**.

An x-ray shows doctors whether a bone has broken. This x-ray shows a broken upper arm.

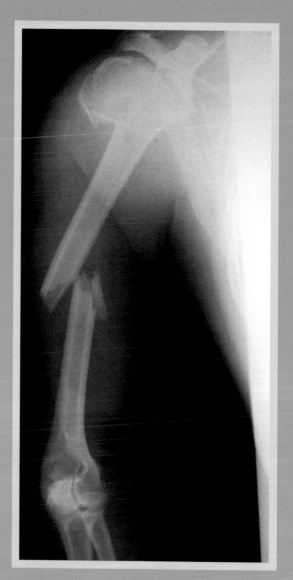

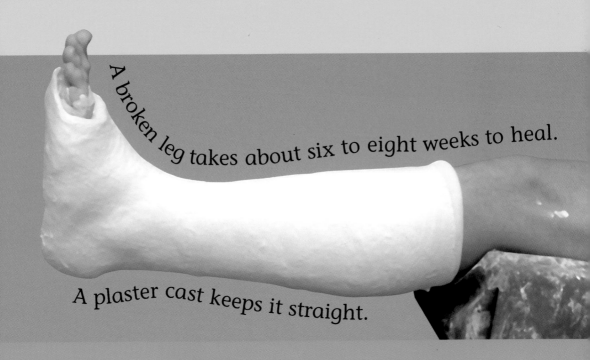

A broken leg takes about six to eight weeks to heal.

A plaster cast keeps it straight.

A bone sometimes breaks into many pieces. This x-ray shows how doctors can put it back together with metal screws and plates.

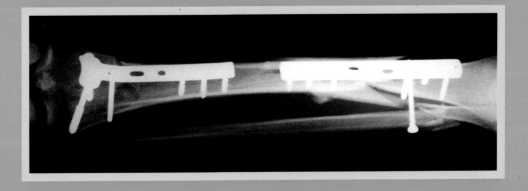

Growing and changing

When you were a baby you had over 300 tiny bones. Some of these were made of a rubbery material called cartilage.

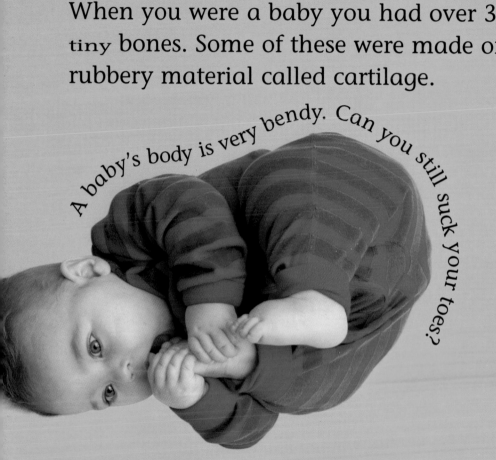

A baby's body is very bendy. Can you still suck your toes?

Over the years, many of the bones join together and the cartilage is replaced by harder, **stronger** bone.

As we grow older, our bones grow bigger.

In older people the bones get THINNER, and joints may begin to feel stiff.

21

Digging up bones

Scientists have dug up remains of animals that have been dead for millions of years.

Their bones didn't rot with the rest of their bodies. Instead, they were changed into stone. These stony remains are called fossils.

This fossil shows the skeleton of a fish.

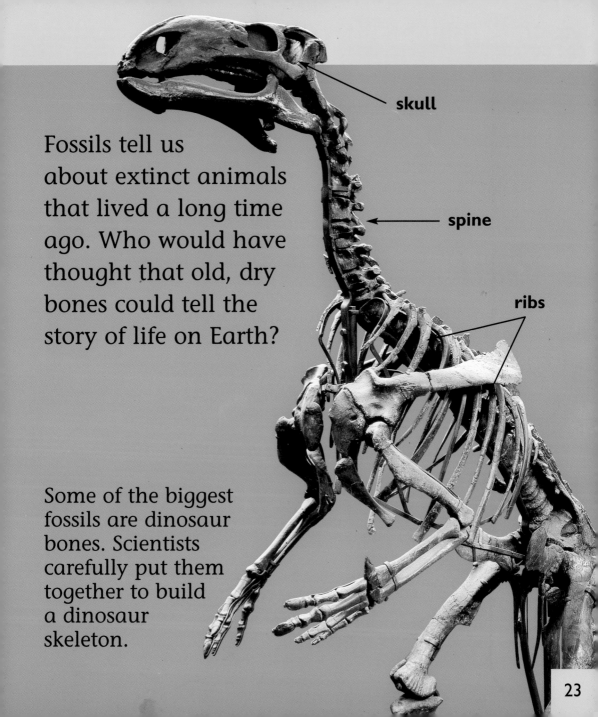

skull

spine

ribs

Fossils tell us about extinct animals that lived a long time ago. Who would have thought that old, dry bones could tell the story of life on Earth?

Some of the biggest fossils are dinosaur bones. Scientists carefully put them together to build a dinosaur skeleton.

23

Glossary and index

Calcium Something found in milk and other foods, which helps build bones. **17**

Cartilage A tough, rubbery material. There is cartilage inside our nose. **20**

Extinct No longer living on the Earth. **23**

Fossil Animal remains from a long time ago, which have turned into stone. **22, 23**

Invertebrate An animal that has no bones inside its body. **5**

Joint A part of the body, such as the elbow, where two or more bones meet. **8, 9, 21**

Muscle A part of the body that pulls on a bone, allowing the body to move. **8, 9**

Organ A part of the body, such as the heart, which has a special job to do. **7**

Vertebrate An animal that has bones inside its body. **4**

X-ray A special photograph showing the inside of a body. **11, 18, 19**

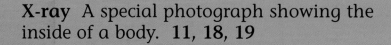